DIGGERS

HEAVY EQUIPMENT

David and Patricia Armentrout

The Rourke Book Co., Inc.
Vero Beach, Florida 32964

PHOTO CREDITS
© Courtesy of Kubota Corporation: cover and page 15; © CASE:
page 8; © Caterpillar Inc.: pages 7 and 17; © Columbus Southern
Power/Ohio Power: pages 4 and 10; © ECS: title page and page 18;
© Q.A. PHOTOS LTD.: pages 12, 13 and 21

Library of Congress Cataloging-in-Publication Data

Armentrout, Patricia, 1960-
    Diggers / by Patricia Armentrout and David Armentrout.
        p. cm. — (Heavy Equipment)
    Includes index.
    ISBN 1-55916-134-5
    1. Earthmoving machinery—Juvenile literature.   [1. Earthmoving
machinery] I. Armentrout, David, 1962- . II. Title. III. Series:
Armentrout, Patricia, 1960- Heavy Equipment.
TA725.A72 1995
629.225—dc20
                                                                    95–3978
                                                                    CIP
                                                                    AC

Printed in the USA

TABLE OF CONTENTS

DIGGERS

Diggers are machines with giant shovels. They do the work that, at one time, was done with a pick and hand shovel. Some diggers are so big they can collect more dirt in one scoop than a person could shovel in a week!

There are many types of diggers. They are built in different sizes and shapes to be used for different jobs. Backhoes, **excavators** (EX kuh vay tors), power shovels, and dredges are all digging machines.

The biggest shovel made was for a walking dragline excavator called "Big Muskie"

EXCAVATORS

Excavators are big digging machines. A tractor engine supports a platform with a rotating cab. The cab is where the operator sits.

Excavators ride on crawler treads that keep them from getting stuck in loose dirt or mud. They have a long arm that is jointed, or hinged, in two or three places. The arm is moved by the operator and supports a bucket for scooping.

An excavator digs a waterway with its large shovel

TRENCHERS

Trenchers are small tractors that can be fitted with different attachments.

The most commonly used attachment looks like the blade, or chain, on a chain saw. The chain has sharp metal teeth that cut narrow ditches. These narrow ditches are called trenches. Workers dig trenches so small pipes and wire cables can be buried underground.

With different attachments, trenchers can be used to dig holes, plow small fields, and load dirt with its shovel.

ncher makes a narrow ditch that
e used for drainage pipes

WALKING DRAGLINE EXCAVATORS

Walking dragline excavators look more like a crane than a digger. These huge machines move slowly across the ground on wide crawler treads.

A digging bucket attached to a cable hangs from the excavator's long **boom** (boom). The dragline is a separate cable that connects the bucket to the base of the machine. The dragline is used to pull the bucket through the earth, scooping huge amounts of dirt.

Walking dragline excavators are used for big projects such as digging **canals** (KA nalz).

The crawler treads on this huge walking dragline excavator move 14 feet with each step forward

11

A tunneling machine called a mole was used to construct a tunnel underwater to connect England to France

THE BACKHOE/LOADER

The backhoe/loader is two machines in one. A wide shovel is mounted on the front. A bucket attached to a moving arm is on the back.

The operator drives facing the front of the machine. Before digging, the operator rotates the seat so it faces the backhoe. When digging, the teeth on the bucket make it easier to dig up chunks of earth.

The operator of this backhoe/loader uses levers to dig and lift the shovel

POWER SHOVELS

One type of excavator is the power shovel. Strong cables and **pulleys** (pul EEZ) are used to raise and lower a bucket. The bucket is attached to the end of a moveable arm.

The largest power shovels are so big that the cab operator sits more than sixty feet above the ground. Shovels of this size are used for mining and digging big holes, such as new landfills.

Diggers are used to load trucks with heavy material like rock and stone

DREDGES

Dredges are floating diggers. Most are used to dredge or scrape mud and other debris from the bottoms of shallow bays. They are also used to widen and deepen shipping **channels** (CHAN ulz).

There are several types of dredges. Suction dredges use air to suck mud through a big pipe. Dipper dredges have a bucket attached to the end of a chain. The bucket drags the bottom of the bay, scooping up layers of mud and **silt** (silt).

Dredges dump their loads onto **barges** (BAR jez) to be hauled away.

A dredge is used to deepen the turning basin of this shipping port

TUNNEL DIGGERS

One of the strangest types of digging machines is the mole. Moles are used to carve or dig tunnels.

Looking like giant screws, cutters on the front of the mole **bore** (bor) through dirt and clay. The earth moves through the machine and onto **conveyors** (kun VAY orz). The conveyors take the dirt and clay to the opening of the tunnel for removal.

The biggest tunneling project ever connects England to France under a stretch of water called the English Channel. The tunnel is 31 miles long and dips as far as 148 feet below the channel.

The mole bores through dirt and clay like a giant screw

THE BIGGEST OF BIG

"Big Muskie" is the largest moving land machine ever built. Used by the Ohio Power Company to excavate coal, "Big Muskie" used more electricity than a small city.

The machine's giant bucket could dig 20 dump truck loads of coal in a single scoop. Eventually smaller, more efficient diggers replaced "Big Muskie."

Glossary

barges (BAR jez) — large flat-bottomed boats usually moved by towing

boom (boom) — an arm that helps to support cables and pulleys

bore (bor) — to make a hole by drilling

canals (KA nalz) — water passages

channels (CHAN ulz) — deep parts of a waterway, usually long and narrow

conveyor (kun VAY or) — a moving belt where items are placed and transferred somewhere else

excavator (EX kuh vay tor) — a machine used to dig or hollow out

pulleys (pul EEZ) — grooved wheels that hold a rope or cable

silt (silt) — very fine earth that floats in rivers, lakes, and ponds

INDEX